CHEESE
LOCKER

FLYINGNUTS

DOUBLE-TALK
Word Sense & Nonsense

Schiffer Publishing Ltd

4880 Lower Valley Road   Atglen, Pennsylvania 19310

Other Schiffer Books By The Author:

Busy Bodies: Play Like the Animals, 978-0-7643-3832-8, $14.99

A to Z Pick What You'll Be, 978-0-7643-3701-7, $14.99

Library of Congress Control Number: 2011941934

Type set in Kids

ISBN: 978-0-7643-3962-2
Printed in China

Schiffer Books are available at special discounts for bulk purchases for sales promotions or premiums. Special editions, including personalized covers, corporate imprints, and excerpts can be created in large quantities for special needs. For more information contact the publisher:

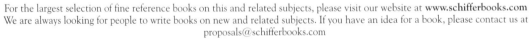

Published by Schiffer Publishing Ltd.
4880 Lower Valley Road
Atglen, PA 19310
Phone: (610) 593-1777; Fax: (610) 593-2002
E-mail: Info@schifferbooks.com

For the largest selection of fine reference books on this and related subjects, please visit our website at **www.schifferbooks.com**
We are always looking for people to write books on new and related subjects. If you have an idea for a book, please contact us at proposals@schifferbooks.com

This book may be purchased from the publisher.
Include $5.00 for shipping.
Please try your bookstore first.
You may write for a free catalog.

In Europe, Schiffer books are distributed by
Bushwood Books
6 Marksbury Ave.
Kew Gardens
Surrey TW9 4JF England
Phone: 44 (0) 20 8392 8585; Fax: 44 (0) 20 8392 9876
E-mail: info@bushwoodbooks.co.uk
Website: www.bushwoodbooks.co.uk

DOUBLE-TALK

Word Sense & Nonsense

Zora & David Aiken

Illustrated by David Aiken

To Eleanor Mae Lynne

Some words are easy,
You know what they say.
Some will surprise you,
Two thoughts come your way.

A **bookworm** likes books,
As you plainly see.
A **book worm** might hide
On page twenty-three.

One **cat tail** twitches,
As kitty cat hides.
A row of **cattails**
Stands tall alongside.

One **drumstick** plays drums,
To help keep the beat.
One **drumstick** tastes good,
A big treat to eat!

One **butter cup** serves
The butter each day.
But **buttercup** blooms?
A golden display!

Dog catchers chase pups
Who run out the gate.
This **dog catcher's** glove
Means out at home plate!

A **keyboard** plays notes
To set the group's pace.
But maybe a **key board**
Keeps keys in their place.

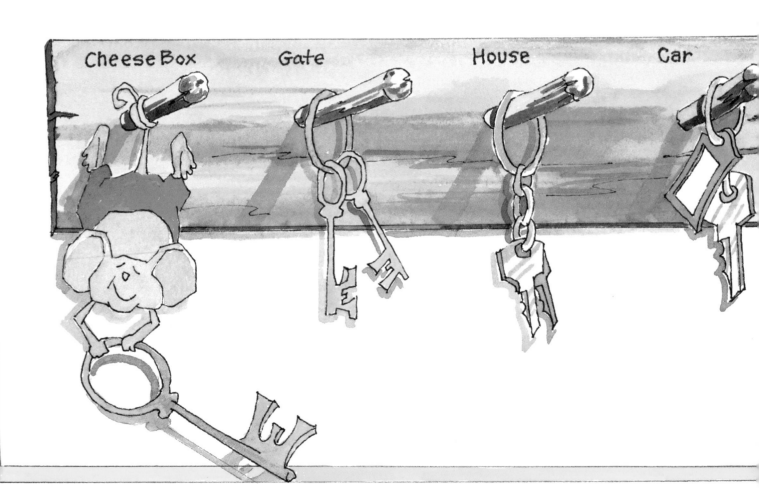

Cheese Box   Gate   House   Car

Watch **flying squirrels**,
They leap and they soar.
(Which **flying squirrel**
Zooms by with a roar?)

Hummingbirds hover,
Then fly out of sight.
Could these **humming birds**
Hum new tunes each night?

The **sandman**, they say,
Might help us to snore.
But not the **sand man**
We build at the shore.

One **blue bell** can ring
A loud wake-up call,
While fields of **bluebells**
Hold flowers for all.

Piggy banks save coins
For rainy days, we say.
Could big **piggy banks**
Do business all day?

A lunch of **fast food**?
A treat any day,
Unless the **fast food**
Tried running away!

Now find some new words
To put in this book.
Draw the new pictures,
And see how they look.